D074467

Market Fresh Mixology

presents

Life, Love, Happiness, & Cocktails

© 2021 by Bridget Albert and Mary Barranco

Market Fresh Mixology Presents: Life, Love, Happiness and Cocktails, is a work of fiction. Any resemblance to actual events or persons, living, or dead is entirely coincidental.

All rights reserved. No part of this publication may be reproduced, distributed, or transmitted in any form or by any means, including photocopying, recording other electronic or mechanical methods, without the prior written permission of the publisher, except in the case of brief quotations embodied in critical reviews and certain other noncommercial uses permitted by copyright law. For permission requests, contact Bridget Albert at www.bridgetalbert.com

Bridget Albert and Mary Barranco
Photography: David P MacDonald, Mikayla Kosicek, and Patrick McShaffrey
Designer: Morgan Krehbiel
Editor: Perrin Davis

To order books, please visit: www.bridgetalbert.com

Hardcover edition ISBN: 978-0-578-35469-9
Paperback edition ISBN: 978-0-578-30967-5

Printed in the United States of America

First Edition

We dedicate this book to you, our reader, and wish you a life of love and happiness.

CONTENTS

CHAPTER TWO
LOVE

CHAPTER THREE
HAPPINESS

INTRODUCTION

Our seventeen-year friendship has led us on a journey that has carried us to the corners of the globe and through countless rich and memorable moments. Our fast alliance and endless conversations often focus on our passion for creating beautiful cocktails, making wonderful memories, and fueling amazing friendships.

In this book, we share recipes inspired by the moments, quotes, fantasies, and stories of our journey in three easy chapters: Life, Love, and Happiness.

Working behind the bar requires a love of cocktails, and no great cocktail is without a story or inspiration. Share in our journey and raise your glass with us in a favorite toast:

"Happiness is like a kiss. It is best when it is shared."

Cheers!

—Bridget and Mary

CHAPTER 1

LIFE

KENTUCKY PUNKIN

"I created the Kentucky Punkin recipe for Clover Club's annual Thanksgiving dinner party. We only close two days a year, so we take advantage of the Thanksgiving downtime and invite our families to join us at the bar. It's become a great tradition that everyone looks forward to." —*Julie Reiner*

1½ ounces 101–proof bourbon

¾ ounce Lustau Palo Cortado Peninsula sherry

1 ounce Pumpkin Biz (½ ounce pumpkin puree and ½ ounce Cinnamon Syrup [recipe follows])

½ ounce fresh lemon juice

2 dashes Angostura aromatic bitters

Orange peel and cinnamon stick, for garnish

Combine all ingredients in a shaker filled with ice and shake until well blended.

Strain into a rocks glass filled with crushed ice, garnish with the orange peel and cinnamon stick, and serve.

CINNAMON SYRUP

½ cup granulated sugar

½ cup water

2–3 cinnamon sticks

Combine all ingredients in a small saucepan over medium heat. Cook, stirring constantly, until the sugar dissolves. Remove from the heat, cover, and set aside at room temperature for 24 hours.

Remove and discard the cinnamon sticks and transfer the syrup to an airtight container. Store in the refrigerator.

JULIE REINER, mixologist and owner of the Clover Club and Leyenda Brooklyn Cocteleria, is a self-described "whiskey girl" who changed the cocktail scene in New York when she opened popular hotspots like Flatiron, Pegu Club, Clover Club, and Leyenda. Clover Club and Leyenda remain among the top bars in New York. Julie rediscovered the Clover Club cocktail, and in her early years in New York, she invented the Hawaiian Iced Tea. She currently mentors other mixologists in their careers, and her book The Craft Cocktail Party: Delicious Drinks for Every Occasion has inspired countless at-home bartenders.

UP AND UP

"What I love so much about learning is that it can happen at anytime, anywhere, and the lessons can come from anyone. One memorable lesson I learned was about a cocktail combination I was convinced would be awful, but it has become my favorite cognac cocktail. The Up and Up is simple and highlights the beautiful complexity of cognac in a subtle and elegant way. I would have this drink at every aperitif hour if it were available." **—Zahra Bates** *Cocktail designed by Trip Sandifer, Atlanta, GA*

2¼ ounces VS cognac	**1 bar spoon Benedictine**
1 ounce dry vermouth	**Castelvetrano olives, for garnish**

Combine all ingredients in a mixing glass filled with ice and stir well.

Strain into a coupe glass, garnish with the olives, and serve.

"I would have this drink at every aperitif hour if it were available."

ZAHRA BATES, who is originally from Los Angeles, receives great joy from learning. Although she felt confident in the experience she'd gained while tending local bars in L.A., Zahra's passion for learning carried her to London to study bartending in depth from 2000 to 2006. Once she arrived there, she focused on refining her finesse.

Now, Zahra's experience includes time spent working behind the bars of Michelin-starred restaurants, and she currently represents a well-known cognac producer.

BRUNCH STARTER

The relaxed attitude of brunch is a reason to savor this switch-up from a classic Bloody Mary. Go way over the top and enjoy all the foods you're craving as garnishes for the savory blend of this mid-morning starter.

1½ ounces aquavit

½ ounce sweet vermouth

3 ounces Clamato juice

Pinch of freshly ground black pepper

Pinch of celery salt

Pinch of smoked paprika

Juice of 1 lemon wedge

Sliders, tater tots, cherry tomatoes, cucumber slices, shrimp, or other brunch foods, for garnish (optional)

Combine all ingredients in a tall glass filled with ice and stir well.

Serve garnished with any or all of your favorite brunch foods!

LAST WORD

This classic cocktail, an answer to your prayer, requires great balance. Back in 1916, the Last Word, a classic pre-Prohibition cocktail, was sold at the bar of the Detroit Athletic Club for 35 cents. Later, the drink made its way to New York City. A lovely balance of sour, sweet, and pungent, the Last Word gets its gentle green color from the Chartreuse. Measure carefully: balance is important in this recipe.

¾ ounce gin

¾ ounce green Chartreuse

¾ ounce maraschino liqueur

¾ ounce fresh lime juice

Combine all ingredients in an ice-filled shaker and shake until well blended.

Strain into a cocktail glass and serve.

Dear God:

Every day is about the people in my life.

I accept that I am a caregiver, born to sacrifice my time for others.

I am asking for the courage to take a moment to myself and not feel guilty.

Help me embrace my body instead of picking it apart.

Help me embrace the quirks that make me the woman I am.

Teach me to simply be.

Teach me to breathe deeply instead of holding my breath in anticipation of what is next.

Help me to live fully in this moment and to stay present in my mind and soul.

Free me to stop managing my emotions to spare others my feelings.

Give me this test of courage that allows me to take care of me first and lets the rest just fall into place.

Amen.

SUMMER IN MANHATTAN FLOAT

Go ahead and let your badass self dive in and indulge with the Summer in Manhattan Float. No need for a cherry garnish with this Manhattan; we've got that covered with a scoop of rich dark chocolate-cherry ice cream.

5 ounces root beer

2 ounces rye whiskey

¾ ounce sweet vermouth

1 scoop dark chocolate-cherry ice cream, for topping

Combine all ingredients except the ice cream in a hurricane glass and stir well.

Add the ice cream and serve.

Dive in all the way

PIMM'S CUP

Sometimes a sturdy, classic British cocktail is just what you need. James Pimm, the owner of a London oyster bar, invented this helpful cocktail sometime between 1823 and 1840. The original version of the Pimm's Cup, which was known as a tonic for health, featured gin, quinine, and various herbs. It was originally served in a special cup known as the No. 1, hence the liqueur's name.

4 cucumber wheels

½ ounce simple syrup

2 ounces Pimm's No. 1

1½ ounces ginger ale

1 ounce fresh lemon juice

Combine 2 of the cucumber wheels and the simple syrup in a tall glass and muddle well. Add the remaining ingredients and ice and stir well.

Garnish with the remaining cucumber wheel and serve.

Why doesn't he call?
Does my phone work?
Did he receive my messages?

Why doesn't he call?
Am I falling too quickly?
Did I share too much?

Why doesn't he call?
Did he mention the next time
    we would see each other?
Where are my boundaries?

Why doesn't he call?

BELLINI

The right blend of prosecco and peach puree to celebrate the color of life. The Bellini was invented in the early to mid-1930s by Giuseppe Cipriani in Harry's Bar in Venice, Italy. The white peaches lend a beautiful light-pink hue to the cocktail with just the right amount of sparkle for celebration.

3 ounces prosecco	**2 ounces white peach puree**

Combine the ingredients in an ice-filled shaker and slowly rock back and forth until blended.

Strain into a champagne flute and serve.

Although anticipated, something about the moment her mother drew her last breath surprised her. Now she was defined as a motherless daughter. How did she move to the front of the line so quickly?

Taking care of her in those final days never made her tired or angry. The final act of caring was just that. A final act.

From that point forward the task became to live a life that that honored all the good in the woman who raised her.

Funny how the empty space has never filled.

It seems it is the color around the empty space that eventually came back into focus.

"You must love and care for yourself, because that's when the best comes out."

−TINA TURNER

BEE'S KNEES

The name of this cocktail, a blend of gin, fresh lemon juice, and honey, is a Prohibition-era slang term meaning "the best."

2 ounces gin

1 ounce fresh lemon juice

1 ounce Honey Syrup (see recipe on p. XXX)

Combine all ingredients in an ice-filled shaker and shake until well blended.

Strain into a cocktail glass and serve.

BEE STING

Bourbon, banana liqueur, honey syrup, and lemon combine into a soothing harmony of flavors in this cocktail.

1½ ounces bourbon

1 ounce Honey Syrup (recipe follows)

1 ounce fresh lemon juice

¾ ounce crème de banana liqueur

Combine all ingredients in an ice-filled shaker and shake until well blended.

Strain into a cocktail glass and serve.

HONEY SYRUP

½ cup honey

½ cup water

Combine the ingredients in a small saucepan over medium heat. Cook, stirring constantly, until the honey dissolves. Remove from the heat, cover, and set aside to cool completely.

Transfer the syrup to an airtight container. Store in the refrigerator.

When you can't find the sunshine, be the sunshine.

MILK PUNCH

Milk Punch was first created in the 1600s and reached its zenith of popularity in the 1800s. The earliest written record of this cocktail's recipe is from a 1711 cookbook by Mary Rockett. None other than Ben Franklin himself created and bottled his own version of this drink.

1½ ounces whole milk

1 ounce cognac

1 ounce dark rum

½ ounce simple syrup

Freshly grated nutmeg, for garnish

Combine all ingredients in an ice-filled shaker and shake until well blended.

Strain into an ice-filled short glass, garnish with the nutmeg, and serve.

The fragrant kitchen carries on the greatest tradition of love and tenderness.

Trust that wherever you find yourself is exactly where you are meant to be.

MARY'S GIMLET

This cocktail was designed to bring Mary's favorite flavors and her favorite spirit, gin, together in a single drink.

5 fresh blackberries

1 ounce Lavender Simple Syrup (recipe follows)

2 ounces gin

1 ounce fresh lime juice

1 sprig fresh lavender, for garnish

Combine the blackberries and Lavender Syrup in a shaker and muddle well. Add the remaining ingredients and ice and shake until well blended.

Double strain into a coupe glass, garnish with the lavender sprig, and serve.

LAVENDER SYRUP

½ cup super fine sugar

1 cup water

¼ cup organic dried edible lavender

Combine all ingredients in a small saucepan over medium heat. Cook, stirring constantly, until the sugar dissolves. Remove from the heat, cover, and set aside to cool completely.

Remove and discard the lavender and transfer the syrup to an airtight container. Store in the refrigerator.

R.B.G.

This cocktail's smooth, rich flavors feature hints of sweetness, and its delicate orange aroma is intoxicating.

2 ounces rye whiskey

1 ounce sweet vermouth

½ ounce mezcal

¼ ounce simple syrup

Burnt orange twist, for garnish

Combine all ingredients in a mixing glass filled with ice and stir well.

Strain into a coupe glass, garnish with the orange twist, and serve.

"Fight for the things you care about. But do it in a way that will lead others to join you."

—RUTH BADER GINSBURG

BOULEVARDIER

This classic cocktail, with its hints of herbaceous flavor and balanced complexity, is simple to make and the perfect accompaniment as you savor the moments that slip by as you dream of success, or as you dream of anything at all. Interestingly, this drink is reminiscent of its more famous gin-based cousin, the Negroni, but the Boulevardier made its debut in 1927, a full twenty years before the Negroni.

1½ ounces bourbon

¾ ounce sweet vermouth

¾ ounce Campari

Orange twist, for garnish

Combine all ingredients in a mixing glass filled with ice and stir well.

Strain into a cocktail glass, garnish with the orange twist, and serve.

"Some people dream of success, while others wake up and work hard at it."

—JULIE MILROY

TELENOVELA

When life feels like you're stuck in a soap opera, take a tequila timeout with the Telenovela. Passion fruit and agave nectar balance the flavors of this cocktail and invite you in, sip after sip. *(Pictured on following page.)*

1 cup ice	1 ounce passion fruit puree
2 ounces fresh limeade	1 ounce silver tequila
2 ounces prosecco	½ ounce agave nectar
1 ounce limoncello	Halved lime wheel, for garnish

Combine all ingredients in a blender and blend until smooth.

Pour into a tall glass, garnish with the halved lime wheel, and serve.

RED HAVEN COCKTAIL

I designed this cocktail for the Taste of the Nation event, which introduced a vodka made from winter wheat grown on a single estate in southern Sweden. The event was coordinated and hosted at Chicago's famous Navy Pier to raise money for the charity NO KID HUNGRY.

The recipe honors the Red Haven peach, which was bred by Stanley Johnson less than 100 miles from Navy Pier. It is hard to overstate the impact this breed had on the quality and availability of peaches around the world. Developed in the 1920s, Stanley's peach provided an important source of both nutrition and income to farmers during the Great Depression. Stanley's niece is a dear friend and former law partner.

---

4 slices fresh Red Haven peach marinated overnight in Red Haven Ginger Syrup

½ ounce Red Haven Ginger Syrup (recipe follows)

2 ounces vodka

1 ounce white crème de cacao

1 ounce peach brandy

1 ounce fresh cream

Freshly grated nutmeg, for topping

Combine 3 of the peach slices and the Red Haven Ginger Syrup in a shaker and muddle well. Add the remaining ingredients and ice and shake until well blended.

Double strain into a cocktail glass and grate the nutmeg on top. Garnish with the remaining peach slice and serve.

"In my view, it is not fair to only contemplate changing bad decisions without first considering the good ones."

—CHRISTOPHER BLOOM,
FRIEND TO THE BEVERAGE INDUSTRY

RED HAVEN GINGER SYRUP

¾ cup dry white wine

½ cup diced fresh ginger

¾ cup water

¾ pound fresh Red Haven peaches

¾ cup granulated sugar

Combine the wine, water, sugar, and ginger in a small saucepan over low heat. Simmer, stirring occasionally, for about 15 minutes, until the mixture reduces to about ¾ cup.

While the syrup is simmering, slice the peaches and place them in a large bowl. When the syrup is fully reduced, remove from the heat and pour the hot syrup through a fine sieve over the peaches. Stir well and set aside for 30 minutes.

The peaches can stand in the syrup for up to 2 hours at room temperature. The syrup can be stored in the refrigerator for up to 1 month. Before using the syrup, remove the peaches.

GIN MARTINI

This classic cocktail is meant to sip and enjoy as it sits majestically on the bar. The original Gin Martini was a sweet drink, as early recipe books called for Italian sweet vermouth, and the dry martini didn't arrive until the early 1900s. When making this cocktail, be sure to use only the finest ingredients.

2½ ounces London dry–style gin

½ ounce dry vermouth

1 dash orange bitters

Lemon twist, for garnish

Combine all ingredients in a mixing glass filled with ice and stir until very cold.

Strain into a chilled cocktail glass, garnish with the lemon twist, and serve.

Most often, she remembered them by their cocktails. Their names faded quickly, but what they drank was somehow memorable.

Theirs was a bold, straightforward encounter, one without finesse. Normally, she would have brushed it off, but this time, it was different in some way. She was left with the impression that he had done this before. He was an artist traveling to an event, and a chance encounter landed them on the same side of the bar. His artistry was creative and thoughtful, with a depth recognizable to even the untrained eye.

She sat and watched him as she sipped her cocktail, just taking it all in. Strong. Sturdy. Handsome. Masculine, with sparkling eyes and the gift of smooth conversation.

The Devil made me do it.

EL DIABLO

Sometimes things just get away from you. Return to your center with luxurious black currant richness from the crème de cassis in this cocktail and the spiciness of its ginger beer married with tequila.

2 ounces silver tequila

1½ ounces ginger beer

½ ounce crème de cassis

½ ounce fresh lemon juice

Lemon wedge, for garnish

Combine all ingredients in an ice-filled shaker and shake until well blended.

Strain into an ice-filled rocks glass, garnish with the lemon wedge, and serve.

BLOSSOMS AND BOTANICALS

"This is my favorite riff on a 50/50 martini, with a cool Japanese inspiration. Perfect to enjoy on a sunny day!" —*Fatima Butler*

1½ ounces Japanese gin

1½ ounces Mancino Sakura vermouth

1 bar spoon Tempus Fugit Kina

2 dashes Hella Ginger Bitters

2 dashes Hella Citrus Bitters

Dehydrated lemon wheel encrusted with Himalayan pink salt, for garnish

Combine all ingredients in a mixing glass filled with ice and stir until very cold.

Strain into a chilled cocktail or coupe glass, garnish with the lemon wheel, and serve.

Oh, let's be adventurers, darling!

FATIMA BUTLER started working behind the bar at the age of nineteen, and at the age of twenty-one, she enrolled in the Chicago Bartending School. Despite the bartending school's promise of lifetime referrals, she applied for hundreds of bartending jobs at bars and restaurants—all to no avail.

This inability to expand her horizons in the bar world led Fatima to a career in the nonprofit world. She and worked her way up to the position of director of operations at a workforce development organization while pursuing a degree in business administration at DePaul University. Over the years, Fatima has held many other positions at nonprofits including grant accountant, operations manager, and even managing director.

In 2018, Fatima decided to return to her passion for bartending and resumed full-time work in the hospitality industry. Many black hospitality workers today face the same struggle Fatima experienced years ago to find jobs or careers that allow them to explore their creative sides. Founding her nonprofit organization Rooted in Hospitality was the next logical step in Fatima's journey: she and the organization share a vision to cultivate a graciously diverse community in the hospitality industry.

CHAPTER 2

LOVE

BRASS RAIL

Mixologist Tony Abou-Ganim created the Brass Rail cocktail in 2007 in honor of the seventieth anniversary of the Brass Rail, a legendary bar in Port Huron, Michigan that was founded and owned by Tony's beloved cousin, Helen David, until her death in 2006. Helen adored B&Bs, so this cocktail would have suited her just fine. At the Brass Rail, Helen could always be counted on to raise her glass in a simple toast: "Happiness!" Here's to love and happiness, Helen!

1½ ounces aged rum

1 ounce fresh lemon juice

½ ounce DOM Bénédictine liqueur

½ ounce simple syrup

1 tablespoon egg white

2 dashes orange bitters

3 drops Angostura aromatic bitters, for garnish

Combine all ingredients in an ice-filled shaker and shake until well blended.

Strain into a chilled coupe glass. Float the aromatic bitters drops atop the center of the frothed egg white and use a toothpick to draw a heart shape through the drops—sexy! Serve.

Here's to love and happiness!

TONY ABOU-GANIM, one of the leaders of the craft cocktail movement, has earned his reputation as "The Modern Mixologist" by bringing the traditional art of mixology into the twenty-first century. Tony is the author of two popular cocktail books, The Modern Mixologist: Contemporary Classic Cocktails and Vodka Distilled.

BELLA ROSE

Deep love is sparkling and sexy—just like this stunning cocktail. Nothing says love like bubbles paired with roses.

2 ounces fresh mixed berry puree

¾ ounce Rose Water Syrup

3 ounces chilled prosecco

Edible flower (such as a rose), for garnish

Place the mixed berry puree in a shaker and add the Rose Water Syrup. Add ice and the prosecco and rock back and forth gently until well blended.

Double strain into an ice-filled old fashioned glass, garnish with the edible flower, and serve.

ROSE WATER SYRUP

½ cup rose water

½ cup super fine sugar

Combine the ingredients in a small saucepan over medium heat. Cook, stirring constantly, until the sugar dissolves. Remove from the heat, cover, and set aside to cool completely.

Transfer the syrup to an airtight container. Store in the refrigerator.

"Anything beautiful is worth getting hurt for."

—PRINCE

Tears rolled down his face as she walked away. She never looked back.

She is now content to know she has felt the passion of true love—a moment that will remain her refuge. She understands that this moment was a transient gift, one that was meant to end.

She has no regrets.

MI AMORE

The bittersweet nature of love is perfectly captured in the Mi Amore.

2 ounces unaged tequila

¾ ounce Strawberry-Infused Aperol (recipe follows)

1½ ounces fresh pink grapefruit juice

½ ounce Honey Syrup (see recipe on p. XXX)

Juice of 1 lime wedge

Club Soda, to fill

Grapefruit twist and lime wheel, for garnish

Build each ingredient in the order listed above to a tall, ice-filled glass and stir.

Garnish with the grapefruit twist and lime wheel and serve.

STRAWBERRY-INFUSED APEROL

4 pints fresh strawberries, sliced   1 (750-ml) bottle Aperol

Place the strawberries in a 2-quart glass jar and pour the Aperol over the fruit (reserve the Aperol bottle). Set the jar aside in a room-temperature dark place for 3 days.

Using a funnel and sieve, return the liquid to the Aperol bottle. Discard the strawberries and store the infused Aperol in the refrigerator.

HIBISCUS ROSEMARY GIN AND TONIC

Enhance luscious moments like this one with the Hibiscus Rosemary Gin and Tonic's fresh citrus and floral flavors and elegant gin botanicals.

2 ounces hibiscus double-brewed tea, cooled to room temperature

2 ounces gin

½ ounce Rosemary Syrup (recipe follows)

3 ounces high-quality tonic water

1 edible hibiscus flower and 1 sprig fresh rosemary, for garnish

Build each ingredient in the order listed above to a tall, ice-filled glass and stir.

Garnish with the hibiscus flower and rosemary sprig and serve.

ROSEMARY SYRUP

1 cup honey

½ cup water

4–6 large sprigs fresh rosemary

Combine the ingredients in a small saucepan over medium heat. Cook, stirring constantly, until the honey dissolves. Remove from the heat, cover, and set aside to cool completely.

Remove and discard the rosemary sprigs and transfer the syrup to an airtight container. Store in the refrigerator.

He was there, sitting on the stairs of the only building in the area and waiting patiently for her. He was leaning back, his legs stretched comfortably before him.

She paused to look at him before he noticed her approaching. He was striking—graying temples, wide shoulders, and a small waist—and as he saw her and got to his feet, she noticed the muscles in his legs and the small red bag in his hand and the blanket draped over his arm.

He ran to her and locked her in a full embrace. She buried her face in his neck and inhaled a combination of soap and the outdoors. Just like that, he pulled away, took her hand, and led her to the rocks overlooking the ocean. She followed, watching his eyes as they walked along.

Swiftly, he spread the blanket over a large, smooth rock and opened the red bag. Inside was their dinner of cheese and bread and libations for them to share.

She silently wished he had not taken his arms from around her.

He raised a glass and handed it to her.

> ## "Certainly, monsieur."
> —THE BARMAN TO JAMES BOND
> IN CASINO ROYALE.

VESPER

The Vesper, a pretty little cocktail we love to love, was first described in the 1953 James Bond novel Casino Royale by Ian Fleming.

2 ounces gin

1 ounce vodka

½ ounce Lillet Blanc

Lemon twist, for garnish

Combine all ingredients in a mixing glass filled with ice and stir until very cold.

Strain into a cocktail glass, garnish with the lemon twist, and serve.

CRAZY FOR YOU

Take a romantic timeout with the Crazy for You.

2 ounces unaged rum

1 ounce fresh lime juice

1 ounce simple syrup

Rose water

Edible flower, for garnish

Combine the rum, lime juice, and simple syrup in an ice-filled shaker and shake until well blended.

Strain into a coupe glass. Spritz the rose water over the top, garnish with the edible flower, and serve.

She was excited by her charming, childlike way. She sat on the grass and invited her to sit next to her.

She kissed her then, feeling both her silky skin and the slight roughness of her lips as she gently placed her lips on hers. She pulled away to catch her breath, smiled, and gazed into her lover's eyes, piercing her soul.

They kissed again. This time, her lips were slightly parted, and she sighed as her delicate tongue explored her mouth. She placed her arms around her, and she could feel every inch of her as she held her close. Their hearts beat wildly in sync.

Suddenly, she withdrew again. They sat that way for a long time, neither one saying a word . . .

I promise to love you all the days of my life ... forever.
That which God has united, no man shall divide.
Damned be the days of doubt.
Yours ... forever and ever.

CHAMPAGNE COCKTAIL

Celebrate life's richest moments with a classic Champagne Cocktail. Champagne Cocktails began appearing in recipe books in the mid–1800s. This recipe is one of the earliest and more traditional versions of the celebratory cocktail, which remains popular today.

1 white sugar cube soaked in Angostura bitters

½ ounce cognac

3 ounces chilled champagne

Orange twist and 1 Luxardo cherry, for garnish

Combine the bitters-soaked sugar cube and cognac in a champagne flute and top with the champagne.

Garnish with the orange twist and Luxardo cherry and serve.

> "Sometimes the heart sees what is invisible to the eye."
> — H. JACKSON BROWN, JR.

BOURBON SOUR

The history of the Whiskey Sour dates back to 1870, when the recipe was published in the Waukesha Plain Dealer, a Wisconsin newspaper. Rich in tradition and flavor, this cocktail is well balanced: warm bourbon, citrus, and sweetness.

2 ounces bourbon

2 ounces fresh lemon juice

1 ounce simple syrup

Lemon wheel, for garnish

Combine all ingredients in an ice-filled shaker and shake until well blended.

Strain into an ice-filled rocks glass, garnish with the lemon wheel, and serve.

THE HONEYMOON

When you want to feel stunning, mighty, and sweet, slip into a Honeymoon.

2 ounces apple brandy

½ ounce orange curacao

½ ounce Benedictine

½ ounce fresh lemon juice

Combine all ingredients in an ice-filled shaker and shake until well blended.

Strain into a coupe glass and serve.

"The best thing to hold onto in life is each other."

—AUDREY HEPBURN

FOG CUTTER

The Fog Cutter, a classic tiki cocktail invented by Victor "Trader Vic" Bergeron, features a blend of spirits, fresh juice, and orgeat syrup.

1½ ounces fresh lemon juice

1 ounce aged rum

1 ounce cognac

¾ ounce fresh orange juice

½ ounce gin

¼ ounce orgeat syrup

1 sprig fresh mint, for garnish

Combine all ingredients in an ice-filled shaker and shake until well blended.

Strain into a tall ice-filled glass, garnish with the mint sprig, and serve.

"Sometimes what you're looking for is already there."

—ARETHA FRANKLIN

THE HIGH PRIESTESS

This cocktail serves up both love and intuition at every table.

2 ounces hot water

2 tablespoons super fine sugar

2 tablespoons instant coffee

2 ounces spiced rum

1½ ounces whole milk

½ ounce maple syrup

In a small bowl, whisk together the hot water, instant coffee, and sugar until well blended. Set aside.

Combine the rum, milk, and maple syrup in an ice-filled shaker and shake until well blended.

Strain the contents of the shaker into an old-fashioned glass. Top with the coffee mixture and serve.

"You've got to learn to leave the table when love is no longer being served."

—NINA SIMONE

STRONG COFFEE

Brew a pot of strong coffee, pour a cup, and savor it as you listen to
Chris Cornell's "Sunshower" on your playlist.

Is sharing a cup of coffee together ever just a cup of coffee?

How they enjoyed their coffee together was always a curiosity to them both, but they had never spoken openly about it. Usually, he would talk about things outside the office—sometimes topics that were wispy and light, and other times ones that were somber.

She could summarize life into a simple azimuth and sort disorder into logical stacks. She knew exactly who he was at any moment, and her clarity was as bright as her eyes. He admired her precision and her strength.

He missed her then, as life carried her back to her family and away from the office. He missed her still.

BLESS YOUR HEART

It might sound sweet as pie, but sometimes "BLESS YOUR HEART" is intended as a sassy insult. You choose.

The Bless Your Heart pairs lovely gin botanicals with fresh fruit flavors. A hint of licorice lends a slight taste of sassy, while the garnish provides fragrant spice aromas.

1½ ounces gin

1 ounce fresh orange juice

½ ounce anise liqueur

½ ounce fresh lemon juice

½ ounce simple syrup

Club soda or seltzer, to fill

Orange wheel studded with whole cloves

Combine the gin, orange juice, anise liqueur, and simple syrup in a tall ice-filled glass. Fill with the club soda and stir well.

Garnish with the clove-studded orange wheel and serve.

LOVE IS LOVE

The Love Is Love is a colorful cocktail filled with tradition, a sweet hint of peach, fresh mint, and bright citrus.

8 fresh mint leaves

¾ ounce peach liqueur

2 ounces bourbon

Lemon soda, to fill

2 dashes Peychaud's bitters, fresh mint sprigs, and lemon wheel, for garnish

Combine the mint leaves and peach liqueur in a tall glass and muddle well. Add the bourbon and ice. Fill with the lemon soda and stir well.

Garnish with the bitters, mint, and lemon wheel and serve.

"I've had to go against all kinds of people through the years, just to be myself. I think everybody should be allowed to be who they are, and to love who they love." —DOLLY PARTON

THE BALLERINA

The Ballerina boasts floral, fruity, and herb notes
in a beautiful choreography of flavors.

1½ ounces reposado tequila

½ ounce sweet vermouth

½ ounce dry vermouth

½ ounce Campari

2 dashes Angostura bitters

Orange twist, for garnish

Combine all ingredients in a mixing glass filled with ice and stir well.

Strain into a coupe glass, garnish with the orange twist, and serve.

"Dance is the hidden language of the soul and the body."

—MARTHA GRAHAM

MODUS VIVENDI PUNCH

"Cocktails are all about sharing and enjoying the people you are with, so I wanted to make a beautiful punch that can be prepared in advance and enjoyed with your friends. The Modus Vivendi boasts a harmony of delicate grapefruit, herbs, and gentle sweetness." —*Katie Renshaw and Daniel De Oliveira*

2 grapefruits

Large ice block

1 (750-ml) bottle prosecco

16 ounces dry vermouth

12 ounces Aperol

12 ounces fresh grapefruit juice

4 ounces elderflower liqueur

4–5 sprigs fresh rosemary, for garnish

Slice the grapefruit into wheels and slice each wheel in half.

Place the ice block in a large punch bowl. Add the prosecco, vermouth, Aperol, grapefruit juice, and elderflower liqueur. Garnish with the rosemary sprigs and halved grapefruit wheels.

Ladle into individual punch cups or short glasses filled with ice and serve.

"Cocktails are all about sharing and enjoying the people you are with."

KATIE RENSHAW was obsessed with cocktails even before she started bartending at the age of twenty-five. When she appeared on the Chicago bar scene, people quickly took notice. Not only did Katie work in some of Chicago's hippest watering holes, she also knew early on that she would one day compete in the United States Bartenders Guild's World Class Cocktail Competition. She competed twice before winning the coveted title in 2019.

HAPP

CHAPTER 3

NESS

CALIFORNIA NEGRONI

"I've put this cocktail on quite a few menus over the years. It's a great 'gateway' to the Negroni: refreshing, light, and so easy to drink. It's a Negroni meets a Gin and Tonic meets a Greyhound."

—KIM HAASARUD

Lime wedge and kosher salt, for rimming

1½ ounces gin

¾ ounce Aperol

¾ ounce ruby red grapefruit juice

¾ ounce fresh lime juice

¾ ounce simple syrup

3 dashes Peychaud bitters

Tonic water, to fill

Orange half wheel, for garnish

Rub half the rim of a tall glass with the lime wedge. Scatter the salt in a bowl and dip the moistened rim of the glass into it. Set aside.

Combine the gin, Aperol, grapefruit juice, lime juice, simple syrup, and bitters in an ice-filled shaker and shake until well blended.

Strain into the prepared glass. Fill with the tonic water, garnish with the orange half wheel, and serve.

Kim Haasarud is the author of the 101 Cocktail series of books: 101 Mojitos, 101 Margaritas, 101 Sangrias, 101 Blender Cocktails, 101 Tropical Drinks, and 101 Champagne Cocktails. The James Beard Award-winning mixologist is well-known for the combination of flavors, textures, aromas, and garnishes of her signature cocktails, which create culinary experiences and celebrate fresh ingredients. When she shared her sunny California Negroni with us, Kim gave us a 102nd reason to love her.

DO IT OUR WAY

The Do It Our Way honors the classic 1970s sitcom Laverne and Shirley, as fun-loving Laverne famously loved the combination of Pepsi and milk. She and Shirley certainly would have agreed that the journey is much more important than the destination. Stay in the moment, and enjoy every step along the way.

3 ounces Pepsi Cherry Vanilla soda

2 ounces unaged rum

1 ounce whole milk

2 maraschino cherries, for garnish

Combine all the ingredients in a tall glass filled with ice and stir well.

Place the cherries on a pick and serve garnished with the cherries.

Enjoy the journey. Worry less about the destination.

We are made of magic and resilience.

RAMOS GIN FIZZ

This classic cocktail was first created in 1888 by Henry C. Ramos at his Imperial Cabinet Saloon in New Orleans. Some say the drink was shaken with ice for more than twelve minutes by an assembly line of bartenders; each would shake it for a minute before passing it to the next. No city is more magical or resilient than New Orleans. Keep on shaking.

2 ounces gin

1 egg white

1 ounce heavy cream

1 ounce simple syrup

¾ ounce fresh lemon juice

¾ ounce fresh lime juice

6 drops orange flower water

1 ounce club soda, for topping

Combine the gin, egg white, cream, simple syrup, lemon and lime juices, and orange flower water and shake well. Add ice to the shaker and shake well again.

Strain into a Collins glass, top with the club soda, and serve.

VICTORIAN HIGH TEA

"When I first came up with this cocktail, I was behind my bar in Louisville, Kentucky. This cocktail takes me back to a time when libations were crafted with love and the people sitting on the other side of the bar were filled with happiness. The reaction to this cocktail always made me feel warm and proud inside. The floral bouquet of the basil and the sharp bitterness of the fresh ruby-red grapefruit juice plays so well together with botanical-rich gin." —*Gary Gruver*

2 ounces fresh ruby-red grapefruit juice

1½ ounces gin

¾ ounce pomegranate juice

½ ounce Hibiscus Syrup (recipe follows)

4 fresh basil leaves

Peel of 1 grapefruit, for garnish

Combine the grapefruit juice, gin, pomegranate juice, Hibiscus Syrup, and 2 of the basil leaves in a shaker filled with ice and shake vigorously for 8 to 10 seconds.

Strain into a rocks glass filled with crushed ice. Pinch the grapefruit peel between the thumb and forefinger of both hands and twist it over the glass to express the citrus oil over the surface of the drink. Garnish with the peel and the remaining basil leaves and serve.

HIBISCUS SYRUP

1 cup boiling water

1 single-serve bag hibiscus tea (about ½ teaspoon)

1 cup granulated sugar

Combine the boiling water and tea bag. Set aside to steep for at least 5 minutes.

Stir in the sugar until it fully dissolves. Set aside to cool to room temperature.

GARY GRUVER is an old-school bartender. After a career of working in bars around the country, winning prestigious cocktail competitions, and representing various brands for the world's largest spirits wholesaler, Gary now leads the cocktail efforts for one of the world's largest hotel chains, but he still enjoys staying close to his cocktail roots.

GALAXY GIRL

Fresh juices splashed into a blend of rum and vodka sweeten the sense of danger evoked by the Galaxy Girl. The drink's name is inspired by the eponymous song on the 2014 album One Way Ride by We Killed the Lion.

2 ounces fresh pineapple juice

1½ ounces citrus vodka

½ ounce mango rum

½ ounce fresh lime juice

4 dashes Angostura aromatic bitters, lime wheel, and pineapple wedge, for garnish

Combine the pineapple juice, vodka, rum, and lime juice in an ice-filled shaker and shake until well blended.

Strain into an ice-filled old-fashioned glass, garnish with the bitters, lime wheel, and pineapple wedge, and serve.

The lounge was dark. The music pumped louder and louder in her head as she moved in unexpected and liberating ways. She closed her eyes and grinded on, allowing the tall, dark, and nameless man with smooth skin and white teeth to move with her. She noticed how fit he was, and how easily he blended into the young crowd.

She wasn't surprised when he slipped her his key, but she knew she wouldn't leave with him. He would know soon enough, but for now, she kept moving . . . and sweating . . . with her eyes closed.

Name the breeze that blows through your hair.

PALOMA

A refreshing switch from the classic Margarita, the Paloma is the most popular tequila-based cocktail in Mexico. Some believe it is named after "La Paloma" (Spanish for "The Dove"), a popular folk song of the 1860s.

2 ounces reposado tequila	**2 ounces grapefruit soda**
½ ounce fresh lime juice	**Grapefruit wheel, for garnish**

Build each ingredient in the order listed above to a tall, ice-filled glass and stir.

Garnish with the grapefruit wheel and serve.

TWILIGHT CRUSH

Live your life like it's a rock musical with this whimsical blue cocktail.

1 cup ice

2 ounces fresh lemon juice

1½ ounces cream of coconut

1½ ounces mezcal

¾ ounce butterfly pea flower double-brewed tea, cooled to room temperature

½ ounce Honey Syrup (see recipe on p. XXX)

Shredded coconut or coconut shavings and lemon twist, for garnish

Combine all ingredients in a blender and blend until smooth.

Pour into a tall glass, garnish with the coconut and lemon twist, and serve.

KIZOMBA

Be a free spirit and get your sexy on!

6 blueberries

6 mint leaves

2 ounces unaged tequila

1 ounce fresh lime juice

1 ounce agave nectar

Lime wheel, for garnish

Combine 5 of the blueberries and the mint leaves in a shaker and muddle well. Add ice and the tequila, lime juice, and agave nectar and shake until well blended.

Double strain into a coupe glass, garnish with the remaining blueberry and the lime wheel, and serve.

OLD PAL

Think only good thoughts while you sip this heartwarming and herbaceous cocktail.

2 ounces rye whiskey

1 ounce Campari

¾ ounce dry vermouth

Combine all ingredients in a mixing glass, add ice, and stir.

Strain into a coupe glass and serve.

What you believe will indeed come true.

CLASSIC NEGRONI

A strong classic. The Negroni was invented in 1919 at the Café Cassoni in Florence, Italy. Legend has it that Count Camillo Negroni asked the bartender to strengthen the Americano cocktail by replacing the sparkling water with gin.

1¼ ounces gin

1¼ ounces Campari

1¼ ounces sweet vermouth

Burnt orange twist, for garnish

Combine all ingredients in a mixing glass filled with ice and stir well.

Strain into a cocktail glass, garnish with the orange twist, and serve.

"Am I good enough? Yes, I am."

—MICHELLE OBAMA

MIAMI VICE

Soaking up the ocean's breeze, sunshine, and a tropical drink can provoke a sense of total vacation happiness. So what could be better than a tropical cocktail? How about two in the same glass? The Miami Vice is a combination of island favorites—a Strawberry Daiquiri and a Piña Colada in the same glass.

2 cups ice

2 ounces unaged rum

2 ounces cream of coconut

2 ounces fresh pineapple juice

1 cup diced strawberries

1 ounce fresh lime juice

Tropical Bird Garnish (recipe follows) or pineapple wedge, for garnish

Combine 1 cup of the ice, 1 ounce of the rum, the coconut cream, and the pineapple juice in a blender and blend until smooth. Transfer to a hurricane glass and place in the freezer.

Thoroughly clean the jug of the blender. Add the remaining 1 cup of ice, the strawberries, the lime juice, and the remaining 1 ounce rum to the clean blender jug and blend until smooth.

Add the contents of the blender to the chilled hurricane glass, garnish with the Tropical Bird Garnish, and serve.

TROPICAL BIRD GARNISH

The right garnish can add flavor, fragrance, and visual appeal to a cocktail. The Tropical Bird Garnish is pure fun with flair!

1 ripe pineapple with healthy green leaves   **Cloves**

Cut 5 green leaves from the pineapple's crown. Select 3 of the leaves and trim them into three different lengths—short, medium, and long. Set aside. (These leaves will be used to make the bird's "wings.")

Place the pineapple on its side on a cutting board. Using a sharp knife, and starting in the center of the pineapple's crown, cut the pineapple in half (1). Repeat, starting at the crown again, to slice the pineapple into quarters.

Select 1 quarter of the pineapple and trim off any excess pulp, creating a straight and even edge (2). Turn the pineapple quarter 180 degrees, so the leafy crown is pointing downward (the crown will serve as the bird's "tail") (3). In the center of the pineapple quarter, make a ½-inch slit to accommodate the bird's "wings." Insert the 3 trimmed leaves into the slit going from shortest to longest.

Trim the tips from the remaining 2 leaves to make a "beak" for the bird. Cut small slits in the new "top" of the pineapple quarter and secure the leaves in them. Press 2 cloves into the pineapple quarter where the bird's "eyes" should be (4).

Cut a long slit into the "bottom" of your bird so it can be slid onto the side of the hurricane glass (it will be heavy, so make sure the glass is large and sturdy).

Position the "bird" on the glass and serve.

PIÑA COLADA

Let the sound of your blender transport you to the islands. The Piña Colada is a tropical summer-and-sunshine treat. This original fun-in-the-sun cocktail was created in at the Caribe Hilton in Puerto Rico back in 1954 by bartender Ramon Marrero.

1 cup ice

2 ounces unaged rum

1½ ounces cream of coconut

1½ ounces fresh pineapple juice

½ ounce fresh lime juice

Pineapple wedge, for garnish

Combine all ingredients in a blender and blend until smooth.

Pour into a hurricane glass, garnish with the pineapple wedge, and serve.

My happy place.

MINT JULEP

In other words, wear your highest hat on top of your tallest hair, and never lose hope.

The classic Mint Julep is strongly associated with the American South. Starting in 1939, serving Mint Juleps became a tradition at the annual Kentucky Derby horse race.

8–10 mint leaves	**2 ounces bourbon**
½ ounce simple syrup	**Fresh mint bouquet, for garnish**

Combine the mint leaves and simple syrup in a julep cup and muddle well. Add the bourbon and some pebble ice and stir well.

Top with more pebble ice, garnish with the mint bouquet, and serve.

REMEMBERING VENICE

This twist on a classic northeastern Italian wine-based cocktail known as the Spritz blends the creamy lusciousness and vibrant colors of white peaches with Aperol and prosecco. Refreshingly simple and rewarding, Remembering Venice is a great drink for making memories.

3 ounces prosecco **1 ounce Aperol**

2 ounces white peach puree

Combine the ingredients in an ice-filled shaker and slowly rock back and forth until blended.

Strain into a champagne flute and serve.

ACKNOWLEDGMENTS

We want to extend a very special thanks all of to the people who have supported us and contributed to a decade-long journey to bring this book to life.

Cheers to:

Katie Shaw, for her energy as our beautiful dancer/model and soul sister;

Nancy "Grandma Diva" Lorenc, for her wisdom;

Cary Jenkins and DDO, for graciously letting us take over their lovely homes for photo shoots;

Our photographers—David P. MacDonald, Mikayla Kosicek, and Patrick McShaffrey—for their creativity and magic;

Our cocktails contributors—Tony Abou-Ganim, Julie Reiner, Gary Gruver, Kim Haasarud, Zahra Bates, Christopher Bloom, Julie Milroy, Katie Renshaw, Fatima Butler, and Christopher Bloom—for their wonderful quotes and cocktail recipes;

Our models for their energy and priceless expressions;

Our designer, Morgan Krehbiel, and editor, Perrin Davis, for understanding our vision for this book and for breathing life into it;

The original SM and storyteller; and

Our families and dear friends, for their ongoing love, support, and happiness.

INDEX

Life, Love,
Happiness,
& Cocktails